THE
DEATH
OF THE
PROPHET

**As Revealed by Almitra
Through Jason Leen**

Revised Edition

**Illumination Arts
Publishing Company, Inc.**

Manufactured in the United States of America.

Cover art:
"The Death of the Prophet" by William Brooks

Library of Congress Cataloging in Publication Data:

Leen, Jason.
    The death of the prophet
    "The powerful completion of Kahlil Gibran's immortal trilogy"—Cover.
    1. Spirit writings. 2. Gibran, Kahlil, 1883-1931.
I. Title.
BF1311.G5L43   1988   133.9'3   88-32021
ISBN 0-935699-02-3

Revised Edition

Illumination Arts
Publishing Company, Inc.
Box 40527
Bellevue, Washington 98004

*This book is dedicated
to God's children everywhere.*

*May it inspire us to soar
to ever-greater heights within the
radiance of the Holy Spirit.*

ACKNOWLEDGEMENTS

Many people have added their love and assistance in countless ways to help bring this work forth. To each of you I offer my deepest thanks—for without your help this reality would still be a dream.

I express my great appreciation to Marisa Lovesong and John Thompson for their invaluable work in preparing this revised edition. Special thanks also to Carol Wright for layout and cover design, to William Brooks for the cover painting which so powerfully welcomes us into this book and to Paula Levine for her exquisite pen and ink drawing at the close.

Grateful acknowledgement is made to Alfred A. Knopf, Inc. for permission to quote from page 61 of *The Garden of the Prophet* by Kahlil Gibran (Copyright 1933) and from pages 119-120 of *This Man from Lebanon: A Study of Kahlil Gibran* by Barbara Young (Copyright 1945).

Above all I express to Kahlil Gibran, to Almitra and to Almustafa my deepest appreciation for this opportunity to be of service. To the best of my ability, *The Death of the Prophet* is presented precisely as you have intended. I know that it will amplify for each reader the brilliant spectrum which *The Prophet* and *The Garden of the Prophet* have radiated over the Earth.

J.L.

PREFACE

Kahlil Gibran stands as one of the most beloved and widely read authors of all time. Through his unique ability to translate timeless, often elusive truths into vivid poetry, he has touched countless lives.

Gibran's motivation was based in Truth and the desire to help all people realize the Truth of their Divinity. He gave form to our innermost, unspoken thoughts and aspirations. And, for many people throughout the world, his words are like a beacon shining in the darkness.

However, his reach extends far beyond the printed page. Often, in published works as well as private letters, Gibran indicated that he was able to penetrate time, envisioning the past as well as the future. To what extent he visited these realms is unknown, but it is certain that this ability greatly influenced his work.

While writing *The Prophet*, Gibran was inspired by an Infinite Source which enabled him to perceive, not only the exceptional quality of the work required for this project, but the totality of the completed work itself. This inspiration became increasingly important toward the end of his life, allowing him to know for certain that his work would be finished, even after his death.

Gibran realized that *The Prophet* was only the beginning. Having seen the whole of the work in his vision, he knew that two more books would be required in order to complete Almustafa's message to humanity.

And so he began the second book, *The Garden of the Prophet*, and worked on that manuscript until the day of his departure. Shortly before dying he wrote:

"I go, but if I go with a truth not yet voiced, that very truth will again seek me and gather me, though my elements be scattered throughout the silences of eternity, and again shall I come before you that I may speak with a voice born anew out of the heart of those boundless silences.

"And if there be aught of beauty that I have declared not unto you, then once again shall I be called, ay, even by mine own name, Almustafa, and I shall give you a sign, that you may know I have come back to speak all that is lacking, for God will not suffer Himself to be hidden from man, nor His work to lie covered in the abyss of the heart of man."*

With this prophetic statement, Gibran boldly disclosed that his writing was truly Divine in origin and that his completed work would eventually be presented in its entirety—even though his physical death was imminent.

More than forty years later, on January 6, 1973, I became an unknowing participant in the fulfillment of Gibran's prophecy. Early that morning, the etheric form of Almitra—an Arabic priestess—materialized in the study of my home. She had come to bring me a story.

This was the silent beginning of Almustafa's

---

*Kahlil Gibran, *The Garden of the Prophet* (New York: Alfred A. Knopf, Inc., 1933), p. 61.

return. Little did I know that I was about to undertake a project which would encompass more than six years of my life.

At that time I was in my early twenties. Having read very little of Gibran's work, I didn't realize the significance of the story or the name Almustafa. Although I had some previous experience with clairaudience, I had never attempted to create a manuscript using this process.

In the beginning, Almitra's visits brought both joy and confusion. It was a very demanding process as, frequently, the rhythm of her words was extremely difficult for me to follow. And for a long time, I had absolutely no idea what title the finished work would bear.

However, one thing was clear from the outset— there was an extraordinary energy present whenever I was receiving the material. It was an uplifting, exhilarating feeling that I had never felt before.

This energy sustained and nourished me throughout the years, as I worked to capture in our limited earthly language the delicate beauty of Almitra's vibrations reflecting the story of her beloved.

By complete devotion to this endeavor, and through a steady growth in my own awareness, the manuscript was finished early in 1979. Later that year the first printing was accomplished.

Through a wide variety of sources, I have sought to validate the truth of this work. Now, each one of you will be able to decide for yourself: Does *The Death of the Prophet* conclude the trilogy as Gibran intended?

I, for one, sincerely believe that it does.

However, I have not been alone in assisting Gibran to deliver Almustafa's song to the Earth. Barbara

Young aided in a similar fashion after Gibran's death by completing the second book of the trilogy, *The Garden of the Prophet*.

Her later book, *This Man From Lebanon: A Study of Kahlil Gibran* describes some of Young's experiences with this process:

"Gibran had originally planned for two additional volumes to complete *The Prophet* series, the one just mentioned, and the third to be called *The Death of the Prophet*. Of the last, unfortunately nothing had been written. He had talked of it often, saying, 'We shall write this, and this.' But only one line was written down. The line was the summing up of the tragic end that he foresaw for Almustafa. It was this: 'And he shall return to the City of Orphalese...and they shall stone him in the marketplace, even unto death; and he shall call every stone a blessed name.'

"It was to have been a book concerned with the relationship between man and God, even as *The Prophet* concerns relationships between man and man, and *The Garden*, between man and nature.

"*The Garden* was, as Gibran said, 'on the way.' The various pieces were practically complete. No arrangement had been planned, however, and the thread of the story on which the jewels of his thoughts were to be strung was missing. And it was some time before I could bring myself to do it. But it finally became crystal clear to me that it was a privilege as well as a compulsion, something I could not get away from, day or night. There was a curious urge that came, tenuous and insistent, out of nowhere, waking me in the deep of night and questioning almost audibly, 'When will you begin?'

"When I did, at last, sit down to mold the book into its final form, there was no difficulty, no hesitation. The frame for the various pictures Gibran had drawn with his glowing words came into being as if he were indeed supplying the need, and so the book was finished."*

I had been working on *The Death of the Prophet* for several years before discovering this information. The immediate impact on me was very powerful; her words provided tremendous support and validation for my own experience. She clearly echoed a number of my deepest feelings and realizations from my experience of working with Gibran.

Yet this process is not unique to Gibran. In the history of literature, there are numerous examples where individuals have felt directed, often compelled, to complete an unfinished work after the author's death.

As the human race is now entering a period of unprecedented growth in consciousness, many people are receiving inspired information and spiritual guidance. It is gratifying to observe that this information is, at last, being more openly accepted by the general public.

This preface is not the place for a full description of the "receiving" process. That is a subject which varies as greatly as the individuals involved. However, I do sincerely believe it possible for any sufficiently-

---

*Barbara Young, *This Man From Lebanon: A Study of Kahlil Gibran* (New York: Alfred A. Knopf, Inc. 1945) pp. 119-120.

motivated person to access enlightened thoughts, concepts, even works of art, which might otherwise be lost to humanity.

Were it not for such a process, this immortal story—Almitra's gift to her beloved Almustafa—would have been lost forever.

Those who have listened to Almustafa's wisdom and loved him will find their hearts renewed in that love, as he once again helps us to hear the sometimes silent Songs of Life.

Jason Leen
August, 1988

THE
DEATH
OF THE
PROPHET

Almustafa, the chosen and the beloved, who was an evening unto his own day, had traveled for many seasons beyond the island home of his ancestors, journeying far into unknown and distant lands.

And amid the progression of those terrestrial seasons there visited his heart a season of a different nature, calling him to return unto the city of his youth.

Thus it was in the month of Ielool, during the season of gathering, that he returned yet a second time unto the city of Orphalese, nine years unto the day from the time of his departure.

His return was that of a man heavily laden with the fruits of his manhood, and so he would have that harvest gathered and consumed with loving hands.

For many days these feelings greeted me as

faithful messengers of his approach. And as it had occurred upon his first arrival, so it occurred now with his return that his form of light visited me in the darkness ere his form of flesh visited me in the light.

And as I had sought him the first time, even so I searched for him now, and thus found him when he was but a little while within the city.

When I first beheld him, he appeared at once both older and younger. For his eyes were softer, yet somehow brighter, and his frame curved more, yet he appeared as enduring as the very earth.

His eyes sought mine as I came near him, and he stood to greet me. Extending his hands toward me, he spoke:

"Almitra, my sister of light! Long has the eye of my mind sought and beheld you amid the movements of your days, and long have the wings of my heart sought and enfolded you amid the dreams of your nights.

"Come, stand closer to me now, that my eyes may bathe in your liquid beauty; and open your heart, that we may once again blend our spirits beneath the heavenly raiment of the stars."

I could do naught save move forward. The words which he had spoken contained the very oceans, and I moved as though carried by strong waves.

Even so, his hands accepted my face as gently as the sea accepts the clouds. Ay, it was with such tenderness that his hands seemed to possess an added life of their own, for they touched my face with sight, like unto the hands of a blind man.

Yet never for a moment could I envision him so. For as Almustafa stood before me, there appeared a light within his eyes which penetrated to the deepest part of my being.

And as the essence of that light touched my mind, the procession of the nine years past gathered within the sanctuary of my memory and prepared to present themselves unto Almustafa.

I made ready to speak, to give life to their various rhythms and forms, but I found myself drawn even deeper within the radiance of his eyes.

And thus I stood silently, feeling my entire being filled with that very brilliance as he spoke to me, saying:

"Know well, Almitra, that I have not come

15

seeking after the spent words of yesterday, nor the unwitnessed passions of the morrow.

"Rather have I come absorbed within the moment, *Now*; for this eternal instant is the birthplace of the ages, and thus it completely contains that which is named time within the infinity of its own timelessness.

"Ay, for both yesterday and tomorrow meet in constant, silent communion in the *Now*.

"And here they blend and pour forth their sparkling wines into the twin vessels of themselves, in silent faith that you shall drink yourself into a languorous sleep and passively accept the yoke which they would place upon you."

"But beware, once that yoke is fitted it is difficult to remove, for theirs is a power both great and subtle.

"Tomorrow and yesterday would appear to you, in your intoxication, as guides essential to your very existence. Yet they do naught save lead you around in cycles, where you are forever weaving the dreams of your tomorrows with the deeds of your yesterdays.

"And so you create a fabric that you wear as though it were your very skin.

"Ay, exceedingly strange are the actions in

16

which they would involve you."

"And all the while that you are absorbed in completing these actions, you continue unaware of the very truth that you are indeed the weaver, as well as that with which you weave.

"For surely you created time, and did so with your movements.

"Yet your various movements have their origin in but one, and that movement is the rhythmical pulse beat of the infinite moment: *Now*.

"Almitra, abandon your attempts to limit Life within the moment. Rather would I have you understand that each moment is a doorway which can lead you into infinite space, space which is brimming with Life."

Allowing me to absorb the strength of his words, he paused before continuing:

"Come, sister, soar with me within this brilliance and move far beyond these clouds of uncertainty.

"Though we darken our minds with thoughts of limitation, we are in truth beyond all limitations.

"And though we find ourselves clothed within these forms, verily we are formless.

"Absorb the light of this Truth, Almitra, and let it nurture you as the sun nurtures the seed, inspiring you to lift your eyes unto your larger Self, who so lovingly awaits you and forever watches over you.

"And within the ecstatic embrace of this inspiration, realize the unity of the smaller and larger Selves.

"Understand that there is but one Self throughout the whole of time and space. Ay, a single source for all things living, the very Spirit of Life itself.

"And likewise understand that once unified within the Spirit, there is no creation in time or space that you cannot attend to.

"And so it should be, for even though you are on the Earth, you are not entirely of the Earth; and you shall come to know and experience the joyous freedoms of space."

With the last of these words, the light which Almustafa had focused within his eyes came flowing out like liquid gold, expanding into a visible sphere that enveloped both of our forms within the aurora of its own.

Unified within the light, we soared deep into the night until the first rays of dawn accompanied our return.

And once within the city we went straightway to the Temple, for one awaited us there with anxious thoughts.

We entered quietly, but with her sensitive ears she heard us; and so she came to greet us in the entrance hall. Warmth and smiles were her gifts as she embraced me, and she continued to bestow them as she moved toward Almustafa.

Turning in the light, she stood before him and softly said:

"I am Sarah."

And for the first time, he could see the evidence of the gift which Life was soon to bear her.

Standing silently for a moment he smiled, then walked toward her and gently embraced her, saying:

"Praised be, O Mother of the Stars, the Temple shall once again bloom forth in flower."

We were silent for a space, and then I spoke:

"Come, let us move into the garden and break our fast, warmed by the radiance of the morning sun."

We seated ourselves between two cypress trees and shared our meal joined in silence, a silence that echoed with the invisible laughter of our childlike joy and the jubilant songs of our larger Self.

Our silence remained unbroken until Almustafa turned toward Sarah and besought her, saying:

"Sarah, even though I have known you only moments, there is that within you which would have me counsel you as though our friendship were ancient indeed.

"And so I ask you to speak to me of that which is caught within your heart, and in so speaking dissolve its influence upon you. Relieve your heart of its burden, enabling it to open instead unto the wonders of joy and love."

His words held a powerful, healing balm for Sarah. And it was with a calmness unknown in her for many months that she answered him:

"Almustafa, many times Almitra has shared her thoughts with me concerning the strength of your vision, yet I am experiencing it now for the first time.

"And it is strange indeed, for you have surely seen into the core of my being, leaving me no space to hide the thoughts that I feel you already know.

"You bid me speak, and so I shall ask you to share with me your gift of vision and reveal unto me the outcome of my days.

"Guide me with your light; for though my eyes once held the light, they are filled now with naught save shadows, shadows of confusion and anxiety.

"Brother, I would know of my days to come, for much has appeared that speaks loudly of change, but knowledge of such movement has yet to appear."

"Almitra has spoken of the cycles within her Temple, telling me that as the time comes for someone within the Temple to leave, yet another appears to take her place; and the two know each other in some special way.

"For nearly two years before I entered these halls, I dreamt of a woman and knew her face as well as my own. And yet, having married a man with little understanding of such things, I kept my dreams unto myself.

"But with the death of my husband this year, I had to seek that face, if indeed it did exist.

"I searched through many cities and villages, and yet I failed to find her. Even so, my heart still guided me to seek her.

"Then, one morning as I sat within the marketplace of this city, she came. And we knew each other as I have known no other.

"Since my arrival she has shared her wisdom with me; and now that you are here and have satisfied her dreams of your coming, she waits only to deliver my child ere she goes.

"But Almustafa, what of me?

"How am I to serve? How can I give what I do not seem to have?

"And what of my child? Is this our home?"

Almustafa raised his hand in a sign of serenity and spoke to her, saying:

"Sarah, be at peace."

He held her silent within his gaze for a long moment and then continued speaking:

"Sister, why do you puzzle at your growth? Know you not that the very Spirit of Life guides your every step?

"Better by far would it be for you to seek communion with the Spirit than to sit and question me.

"Only the Spirit can reveal unto you the secrets of your heart. And the treasures which you seek are surely hidden there, rather than within the movements of your days.

"Remember, Sarah, that the days of every world are numbered, while the wonders of the heart are infinite."

"When you reveal the secrets which you hold, I am sure that many treasures will be shared indeed, for you are like unto the seed from which this forest grew.

"In your youth, you do not yet conceive of the life which shall spring from within you as the tree springs from within the seed.

"And as you grow to become the tree, you do not remember yourself as the seed.

"Thus, unable to complete the circle of your own existence, you are unable to understand the completed sphere which is Life.

"Without conceiving of the whole of Life, you live only within the fragmentary world of your own understanding.

"And your growth is limited to the height

that you envision having in which to grow, just as the tree is limited in its height by the depth to which its roots penetrate into the earth."

"Sarah, you may view the entire universe and yet, failing to understand the unity of all things, your viewing comes to naught.

"At best you obtain but a partial glimpse of that which you sought to see; for without the light of unity to illumine your vision, you perceive naught save darkness and shadows.

"But know well that your understanding of the universe must first be born within yourself and include the many varied natures of the Self. For only through your understanding of the Self shall you understand the universe.

"Ay, Sarah, you need but to grow and experience your Self."

"Even so, seek you to be in your growth more like this tree under which we sit. For even as a seed did it release the life within it; and so must you release yourself.

"The seed did not fear of how it would grow, nor where, nor what, nor when it would grow. It did naught save *release* itself, and yet it did grow.

"And singing of Life, it consummated the

sacred union of the earth and sky.

"For this tree is little else but earth and sky. Earth that has lovingly lifted itself into the sky, seeking the caresses of the wind and rain, and sky that has plunged itself deep into the Earth, seeking to caress her very core."

"Ay sister, more like unto this tree I would have you become; and yet even now you are like unto it in many ways that do not pass unheeded.

"For does not the tree, as a seed, need to cast off its shell ere it is able to rise into the sky? Even so will you cast off your shell ere you rise from out of your seed Self unto your sky Self.

"And likewise, does not the tree need to stretch its roots deeply into the earth before it can lift itself majestically into the sky?

"Even so do you need to tap the very depths of your being, ere you shall be able to rise unto the heights of your being.

"And Sarah, is not the tree in constant, joyous communion with all of the elements necessary to its growth? Does it not receive with equal pleasure both the cool, moist kiss of the rain and the fiery hot kiss of the sun?"

"Even so, I say unto you that you are eternally surrounded by that which you need for your growth.

"Could you but experience this Truth, opening wide to receive the gift it bears you, all memory of separation would fade, leaving only the shining song of unity to vibrate through the whole of your being.

"Bathed in this song, even death does not stop you. For death is transformed into Life, who stands before you only to serve you, not to contain or detain you.

"No longer need you fear the face of death. Free yourself, Sarah, and love her. And in so loving her, be freed of any pain which you might have claimed as extra measure with her gift of growth.

"Be at peace, knowing that you are ever growing toward your larger Self. And understand that you are changing naught save that which need be changed in order to nourish your growth."

The joy of his words found a home within her heart; and so Sarah found herself resounding with the ecstasy of their rhythms.

And she was able to feel the amazement of the seed as it pushes up through the last snow crystals of winter to be welcomed by the incredible fire of the sun.

26

On an evening soon after his arrival, as Almustafa and I sat upon a hill near the city, a small group of men approached us, seeking him.

And as they came near, he studied them in remembrance of the youth they had shared with him, for they were now men and had somewhat forgotten their youthful days.

When they had stopped he stood to welcome them. Each greeted him as master and was greeted in return.

Almustafa was silent for a moment, letting each man savor his reunion in peace; then he spoke to them, saying:

"Pleased I am to meet you here this evening, but I would have you greet me as *master* no longer. Rather would I be greeted as your brother, for I now understand that it is as brothers that we meet.

"Verily no being upon this Earth is

removed from any other, save in the distance of fear. Thus, I ask you to lay aside your fears and let us quickly traverse any distance which might continue to separate us."

He stood silently as the men looked one unto another, seeking a voice with which to give their reply.

At last one man stood forth and said:

"Brother, would that we were beasts of burden, then perhaps we could lay aside our heavy loads; but it seems that our fears are not so easily released.

"Even so, we seek you here now as we sought you many times before: in need of your guidance and knowledge."

Almustafa turned toward them, and his voice shared the freedom of a thousand birds in flight, as he said:

"Brothers, gladly would I counsel you, but how am I to answer you? Should I say 'Nay', you would deem me a miser with my light. And yet, should I say 'Ay', I would but guide you unto your Self.

"For in truth there is naught save that very Self throughout the whole of Creation."

Pausing for a moment, he motioned for them to sit near us; and once they had done so he continued speaking:

"It is only through understanding the Truth of Self that you shall find peace within the ever-flowing stream of Life.

"Verily it is this peace, wearing the cloak of knowledge, which you seek even now.

"And know you well that beating within the heart of the Self is the rhythm from which all other rhythms are created. Better by far would it be for each of you to listen to this single rhythm, and thus tune the rhythms of your own heart closer unto it.

"For so you would reclaim your birthright and live in harmony with Life. You would understand that the Self is infinite, and realize that to turn from its door is to don the yoke of separation and to impose a burden upon yourself that you were not meant to carry."

Consoling them all with a smile, he continued:

"Brothers, seek you to be more like unto the seasons of the Earth; for, in truth, does not each season contain within itself all of the precious secrets of the other three?

"And so would I have each of you do likewise. I would have you unfold yourself until you contain the whole of Life.

"Ay, from the invisible movements of the stars to the invisible movements of the particles of light that fill the very air you breathe, I would have you unfold to embrace infinity.

"Yet now, even in your forgetfulness, you do naught save this.

"Ay, for even though I would have you become more like the seasons in your conscious deeds, you are now like unto them in ways that move deep within your unconscious realms.

"For I say unto you that even though you may move in silent bewilderment, and are at times completely unaware of your very movements, you do indeed move."

"Thus, like unto all creatures who merge themselves with the movements of the seasons, you shall come to sit at the board of your larger Self.

"And at that table you shall be filled with nourishment for your spirit and your body as well.

"So shall you understand the abundance of Life and release yourself into Life's loving care, knowing that whenever you hunger, whatever the source, you have but to open your heart and reach out with your mind.

"Verily, within your reach you shall find that which shall end your hunger.

"And thus you shall realize that each of us stands upon this earth complete of every answer to every question we shall ever ask."

Almustafa suddenly stopped and paused for so long a time that a voice from amongst the group besought him, saying:

"What of the real treasures of your mind, Almustafa? Have your words truly revealed your knowledge to us, or have you kept some secrets hidden?"

Almustafa raised his head and answered:

"Brothers, seek you not the bondage of knowing; seek you rather the freedom of *being*."

"And above all else, my friends, seek not to house within your minds that which does not dwell within your hearts.

"But know you well that the forces and feelings dwelling within your hearts shall display in your minds the entirety of their natures, even as the feelings of my heart have been revealed within my words this evening.

"Verily, you need but unveil the unity of your Self to understand its freedom."

"Ay, you needs must find rather than continue to search; for in that finding all of your dreams shall come home to rest, and you shall finally have the peace that you seek.

"And even though you be forever carried onward in the never-ceasing flow of Life, you shall struggle not; for you shall realize that all is as it should be.

"And within the sanctuary of that peace, you shall behold all of Life's precious mysteries. And passing far beyond the walls of understanding, you shall drink your fill of the beautiful and delicious wine of Life."

"And so, my brothers and my friends, how may I come unto you?

"You are as fields well warmed and watered, which now need only the loving hands of the weeder and the gatherer.

"Surely, through the weeding of your fields, you shall gain the strength and the desire to gather and consume the harvests thereof."

As Almustafa finished speaking, the spell which his words had cast upon the men faded. Even so, each man looked long upon him, and moved only as they gathered to embrace him.

Then, as before, one man stood forth to voice their common feelings:

"Almustafa, your words have transformed the desolate regions of our hearts into the gardens of our souls. Surely no one can ask for more than this; and likewise, no one can give words to our gratitude for having experienced it. Thus we can only bow our heads and say good night."

With this farewell, the men departed as quietly as they had appeared.

After a moment I turned toward Almustafa and besought his eyes with my own, as my words sought his heart. And I said:

"Brother, what of those with withered limbs and weakened forms? Would you seek to minister unto everyone with your words alone?"

He gathered my hands into his and spoke to me, saying:

"Sister, to observe the Truth in every movement, in all of her subtle beauty, and to know the Truth in every form, in all her vital grace, one must search beyond the surfaces of those movements and forms.

"And even now it is so; for I say unto you that were you to know the Truth of our meeting here this evening, you would surely understand that each of those men was cared for in a manner

33

that delivered him from his needs.

"Verily, everyone here tonight received the jewel which he sought."

"And so it is and shall be with all who seek me, for even in their affliction, the waters of Life are nestled around their roots and long only to be summoned.

"Ay, for it is unto naught save their whole Self that I guide all who seek me. Truly all must start upon this journey, Almitra, for I shall not always be here to satisfy their needs."

He raised his head and beckoned me to gaze as he did upon the stars, saying softly:

"What a pity it is that humanity in its haste to obtain some partial knowledge of Life, ignores the truth of its complete and eternal union with the whole of Life."

He was silent then and seemed to be suspended between Heaven and Earth, while he stood looking upon the stars. And as he watched, there appeared a light within his eyes that was no less then the light of the brightest star.

And on another evening Almustafa and I ascended the hills near the city to gaze upon the heavens undisturbed.

It was then that he spoke to me of the Living Breath which envelopes the Earth.

Bowing his head for a moment, he clothed himself entirely in silence as he sought to merge the rhythms of his own breathing with the movements of the air which swirled about us.

And as he stood before me, the wind gathered his cloaks and spread them in the air, forming two wings of light. Thus he appeared to me as a winged angel descending from some ethereal region.

I beheld the light of the heavens around his shoulders and within his eyes as he turned toward me and said:

"The air above the Earth is in constant motion, an ocean of invisible Life. And so it is likened in many ways unto the watery oceans which float upon Earth's surface.

"The Spirit of Life breathes its luminous Breath into both oceans with equal love. And with that very love, both move about the Earth, constantly giving of themselves to sustain life upon this world.

"And with great tenderness and mercy do they minister unto our needs.

"For the oceans bathe and caress our minds and bodies with their rythmic waves, while those airy seas that roam the sky lift our spirits far beyond this world.

"Thus they both connect the smallest of living forms with the vastness of formless Life. And in so doing they complete the circle of Creation, which in harmony sets them free."

"Would that we were as free, for we stand with our feet bathed in water and our hands extended into the sky; yet we cannot breathe within the water, nor can we swim within the sky.

"We would deny the unity within ourselves and thus deny our unity with the whole of Creation.

"But Almitra, change must surely come. Indeed, we must love and devotedly reaffirm this vital union, for only by clothing ourselves with the splendor of this unity can we commune with the Sacred Heart of Life.

"And only through this communion can we experience one of Life's most precious mysteries, and come to understand that there moves within each particle of Life a heart as illumined with love as our own.

"It is this heart which blazes, creating a star from each particle of Life; and it is naught save this very light of Life which we seek with every sip of water and every breath of air.

"We would return into the arena of Life clothed in light once more, and yet we remain outside the gates."

"Can we not learn from the air and the water? The air would swim within the water and the water would float within the air, for they are unified with the whole of Life.

"We would fill our mouths with cool spring water and our lungs with fresh mountain air, yet our eyes remain blinded to the light of love and our ears deafened to the song of light.

"We would drink and breathe of this world and yet remain dead unto the mysteries of Life; for to come alive unto those mysteries, we needs must drink and breathe of Life itself.

37

"Even so, when we understand that every thirst stems from a single thirst for Life, we shall surely drink more deeply of Life, knowing that in doing this we are satisfying all of our thirsts."

With the song of his words fading into silence, he turned his face toward the stars and let his breath merge once again with the air, which moved around us softly now, singing a lullaby of love.

We stood long upon the hills that evening, for it seemed as though the air transported us into a world of a thousand years hence.

And it was from there that we watched the years gather together and float by as though they were formed of clouds.

It was there also that we drank of the mystical draught of time and space. And, soaring beyond them both, we were free.

Thus I was able to perceive the rarer mysteries of the air, which even Almustafa had not spoken of, for they cannot be shared by words alone.

Enraptured by these visions, I soared through endless aeons until at last Almustafa turned toward me and said:

"Sister, there is one who needs our help in the valley below. Come, let us go."

Upon hearing these words I turned toward the valley and tried to penetrate the darkness in search of the one who needed us.

Yet I beheld naught save the dancing of the trees in the wind and felt naught save the gentle fingers of the wind as they caressed my face.

Almustafa perceived my efforts and spoke to me softly, saying:

"Almitra, worry not; it is but a darkened candle which must needs be reignited."

Soon we were led through the valley by the gentle crying of a child. And we followed that song of sadness until we came upon a small boy whose name I knew to be Joshua. He was the youngest son of a tanner within the city and was known by everyone for his adventures amid the surrounding hills.

It was said that he went out amongst the hills by daylight and then fell asleep from his playing, only to wake at the fading of the sun. He would then attempt to race the sun back into the city.

But since he was small and the path very rough, he nearly always failed. And so he found himself alone in the darkness on many a night.

Thus we found him, huddled into a ball and crying in fear and loneliness. Seeing this,

40

Almustafa bent down and lifted Joshua unto himself.

He stood with that great light blazing within his eyes and began singing a song of old, known to bring peace and comfort unto those in need.

Thus Joshua regained his peace and was able to hear the words which Almustafa spoke unto him:

"Joshua, my little brother, why is it that you cry? Can you not see that it is naught save your tears which darken the night? And that it is but your fears which give form and life to the shadows amid the trees?

"You have nothing to fear, brother, nothing to fear of the night which bears the dawn, for there is naught within the darkness that is not also within the light.

"And there is naught within the vast realms of light and dark that is not also within the infinite domain of the Self.

"And since you would play and laugh while the fire of the sun ignites the air at noontide, then continue with your dancing and laughing even as the cool breezes of night tend to the needs of their brothers and sisters who were caught in the heat of the day.

"Brother, go upon your way knowing that

41

even within the darkness of night, the light of Self shines on. You have only to open your heart and eyes to perceive it."

With these words surrounding him, Joshua turned and moved on through the valley. He walked calmly and at peace with the darkness, for his mind was full of starbursts and his eyes were full of light.

And so he appeared to walk on air, full of his new-found love for the night.

And on a morning as Almustafa and I returned from the marketplace, we found Sarah awaiting us. She glowed as the sun poured down upon her and offered us her hands to aid her in rising; whereupon she embraced us both tenderly and smiled, saying:

"The time has come for the little one within me to come into this world."

As I made ready the place of birth, Almustafa knelt before her and spoke to her softly:

"Sister, enlarge your heart so that you may dance to the rhythms which are singing now within you. Ay, give yourself completely unto them, for these rhythms are naught save your child's dance of Life.

"Sarah, move with the child and the rhythms shall enfold you, for the movements of the child within you do naught save complement the very movements of your form without.

"And so it should be, for you are now joined together in performing the Celebration of Birth.

"Unfold yourself within the waves of rhythm; release yourself unto the ecstasy of the dance."

"The moment soars through eternity when the child shall move from within your womb unto your waiting arms.

"Even so, I would have you understand that in that movement the child is but moved by the Mother of Life from one breast unto yet another.

"Stretch out your arms, my sister, so that you may call the breath of Life deeply into you and thus be made ready for the arrival of the child, this sacred star from the deepest of space, who even now soars across the heavens unto your trembling arms.

"Sarah, accept the nourishment of the Spirit and be made strong, for the child within you trembles also and seeks release.

"Be not afraid to open your heart and mind as well as your eyes, so that you shall have full vision, for you are giving birth to a glorious life."

Upon hearing these words, Sarah stretched wide her arms and called forth the breath of Life to enter her womb. Thus, Almustafa and I made ready to deliver the child into the world of earth and air.

Then, even as we prepared, the child presented her head unto our waiting hands. And so we escorted her into this world.

Lifting the child gently onto Sarah's breast, Almustafa spoke unto her lovingly, saying:

"Rejoice, Sarah, at the birth of this beautiful girl; the very ethers adorn her dance in majestic wonder. Surely in her coming she has brought you many gifts.

"But know you well that even though you are her mother and she now comes unto you as a daughter, you shall make no claims upon each other—nay, not even those of love.

"For there is naught of possession in the act of giving birth and in the sharing which follows. There is only the flow of Life moving on, and in that flow there is only love moving, forever seeking a more complete union with itself."

"Even so, sister, this unity shall visit you here on Earth, and you shall feel its presence as you experience the sweet unity of family.

"Ay, and passing far beyond the man-made meaning for that word, you shall realize that the family is much more than a closeness of kin or a gathering out of convenience and circumstance: family is the relation of one loving heart unto another.

"Once that relation is truly understood, the whole of Creation shall be bathed in the very light which has soared from the deepest of space to ignite your heart.

"And thus, Sarah, the whole universe shall be consumed by that flame and naught shall remain save love. This very love surrounds us ere we are born and, likewise, naught save this love truly nourishes our lives."

"For even as you give birth unto your children, so shall they continue to be born anew unto the universe as each moment is born anew.

"And in that perpetual rebirth they are forever surrounded by love.

"Verily, as they came dancing the dance of Life, so shall they continue to dance throughout the ages. Ay, for even as another has promised you, your life is without end."

"Yet seek not to understand nor control the patterns of your children's dancing, nor become afraid when you can no longer hear the tune to which they step.

"Rather would I have you relax your heart in peace, knowing that they dance but to the very music which has moved you—and that their movements have but altered themselves to better suit the nature of the dancer.

"And become not consumed by sadness if your children's dancing should cease to be, for know beyond any doubt that the dance of Life continues on even though the dancer's steps are silent.

"If you could but fathom this, you would be swept up in that very movement and soar beyond the boundaries of life and death."

"For you are Light, created by Light from the essence of Light; and that which you create is Light.

"Even as you give birth and the child moves from within your womb into the air of this world, it is but Light issuing from Light into Light."

On another morning, as Almustafa and I sat within the portico of the Temple talking of his return, a priest named Jataz approached us and besought Almustafa:

"Master, I would speak with you."

Almustafa raised his hand to silence Jataz, saying:

"Surely, I shall speak with all who come before me, but now only as a brother; for I no longer need hear the sound of master to convince me of who I am.

"Ay, no more would I have us be apart; rather would I remember the birthright which we share."

Jataz was silent for a space, as if perplexed, trying to understand these words. And then he said:

"Gladly would I have us be brothers, and yet a word makes us not so."

49

Almustafa lifted his eyes to meet Jataz's and answered him, saying:

"I would not be called brother in name only; rather would I be received within that brotherhood which surpasses all names. For everyone who shall welcome me therein shall understand the truth of our relationship.

"And thus, Jataz, could you but receive me there also, you would indeed know that we are brothers. For are we not both children of Life, born of the same womb of love and created of the same light?"

Upon hearing these words the priest stood as if to go, but instead he turned toward us and said:

"Brother, we have known of your return for only a short while. And so, I have been sent to seek you out and bid you come and share with us our Day of Plenty, so declared to celebrate the overabundance of our fields this year.

"There shall be those of our Temple who come from afar with gifts for all; and although your words sound strange to my ears, some wish you near to speak unto our guests."

Almustafa answered him, saying:

"Tell me, Jataz, who amongst your faith

50

have found within their minds the wisdom to separate the days, declaring some days holier than others?

"Is it in jest, or do they sincerely think that they can add or subtract from the unity of the *Moment*? Do they not understand the Truth of their faith?

"They do naught but subtract from all other days that which they would add to their sacred few.

"Nay, brother, I shall not attend. For not until all of this talk of sacredness and celebration ends shall any one amongst you know what those words truly mean.

"Ay, for as long as any would bless one day and curse another, they know naught of the Truth of days. Thus they understand not that all days are as one day, even as all moments are united and all of Life lives to share one heart."

"Life is forever One, Jataz, knowing naught of the divisions that mankind would place upon it. Nor would it be divided, for it is only mankind that divides itself, and so denies Life's many gifts.

"Let all heed their divisive deeds, lest they should split their very being in twain, losing their ability to function as a whole. And let these

51

be changed instead into deeds of unity, so that the Earth may forever feel the gentle caress of naked feet upon her grass.

"And let there be naught save love in that touching, for love is infinite, beyond all boundaries. And love shall remain long after the grass, and even the Earth itself, is scattered throughout space."

Jataz spoke with fear in his eyes:

"Brother, be silenced lest you should go too far, for I have been trained to report such words as you have spoken. And I fear the results should certain people come to know your thoughts."

Almustafa answered him, saying:

"Nay, I have no fear of such as those. For I have spoken naught save Truth from the first, and I shall continue to speak naught save that very Truth until the last.

"There is no distance I would not travel to share the Truth with those I love; there is no space I would not span to return light unto darkness; and there is no resistance I would not endure to call back Life into a stagnant mind."

At these words, Jataz turned and moved down the steps as though blown by a strong wind.

As he left us he was arrayed in fear and confusion, for his heart had felt the Truth in Almustafa's words. And yet his mind would not be emptied of the beliefs he had known as a priest, beliefs which now battled with the Truth and blocked its passage into his heart.

With sadness in his eyes Almustafa turned toward me and spoke:

"Is it always to be that mankind must prepare against the coming moment? Will there never exist a space or time when all shall release unto Life each moment, exactly unto their needs?

"I pray that it may be so—and soon—for only then shall mankind be made full of the understanding and the desire to continue upon its way.

"Sister, Life is forever with us, forever giving, forever loving. When will that be enough for those who seek to rule the day?"

And on an evening as we made our way high into the mountains to share the grandeur of the heights, Almustafa stopped to speak of the quietly falling snow.

His voice filled the cold night air with warm music, as he said:

"Sing to us, our crystal brothers and sisters.

"Sing to us of your life within our mother sea.

"Kiss our flesh and return once more unto liquid; touch our hands that we may share with you this joyous reunion, for we also were once of the sea. And still do we bear witness unto that union by the rhythms quietly ebbing and flowing within us.

"Sing to us that we may know of your journeys within the sky; anoint our heads that we may share with you this sacred night.

"So kind and full of love our mother proves

to be, that she would send you here to rest and sleep upon this frozen ground to await the heat of summer.

"And then she calls you back into her arms, asking you to give of yourselves to end the thirst of all whom you greet along your way.

"Ay, so very gracious is our mother sea, and tireless in her service, for she gives so much and continues to give until all have filled their needs."

"And yet it should be so, for our mother is infinite in her compassion; and thus she cannot find contentment in fulfilling the needs of one of her children while yet another has needs unfulfilled.

"Even so, Almitra, pity the sons and daughters should they ever turn their backs upon their mother; for in so doing they would signal the end of the very world that she has so lovingly provided for them."

Almustafa then took my hand and guided me through the night. And it was not long before we stood at the entrance of a small refuge nestled tightly amongst the trees, awaiting travelers in the night.

Almustafa opened the latch upon the door

and spoke to me with these words:

"Sister, enter in and find comfort for the night. I would remain here in the snow yet a while longer, but you are weary and must needs rest; and it would please me if you should enter in and sleep."

Knowing the truth of his words, I met his eyes and gently touched his hand, then entered the shelter filled with peace.

Awakening in the morning, I found myself to be as alone as when I fell asleep; and so I moved outside to search for Almustafa.

The snow fell very quickly, and thus my sight was limited; yet within a short space of time I found him. Covered with snow, he stood completely still and uttered not a sound as I came near him.

My heart remembered the kind words he had spoken to the snow; and yet my mind cried out in fear for his life.

As I brushed the snow from his face he startled me with speech, for I had thought him frozen and incapable of movement.

Yet he raised his hand as he spoke to me, saying:

"Nay, Almitra, do not brush away these

brilliant crystals, for they would soothe and refresh me with their pure white color.

"Indeed, are not all colors hidden within their light? Ay, and so they would bathe me in the profusion of the rainbow.

"And as they would refresh me, so shall they in time refresh the Earth."

"The sea lies beyond us in her understanding of our needs and the needs of the Earth. Her liquid love is the Earth's life, forever renewing itself and escorting each season in its turn into the royal palace of *being*.

"Ay, and so it is even here, for these are but the gentle waters of the oceans, dancing very slowly that they might preserve their liquidness until it is needed.

"Yet, sister, there is a fire which burns on, even within snow, that serves to keep me warm. Could you but take one step past this frozen whiteness, you would surely feel the warmth of that fire."

"As all of Life is united, nourished by a single heart, even so, is there not also but one light which illumines all of Creation?

"And being united with the Greater Light, can I not find my way within all realms of Life, which in truth are naught save various realms of myself?

"And thus, can I not embrace the fire which forever burns within this crystalline fragment of our mother sea, and fly within the caress of that fire unto the tropical isles of yet another world?

"Ay, Almitra, even space shall produce no distance, for in truth all worlds are as one world, even as all of Life is united.

"Could you but come to love yourself and all of Life as one Life with undivided love, then you would find yourself one with all of Life, eternally undivided and eternally indivisible.

"Ay, love is the key to the door of Life, Almitra; and once inside that door, the house of Life is filled with love.

"Could we but open that one door, all other doors would forever open unto us."

On another evening as we traveled back into the city, we stopped along our way to rest and partake of our evening meal.

I sat in silence, soothing my tired body ere I ate, while Almustafa gathered wood to make a fire.

And having gathered enough, he turned toward me and spoke:

"Sister, open your eyes, for I would share with you the wonder of this sight. Ay, Almitra, wondrous and sacred; for though fire is common now amongst all peoples, even as it illumines the darkness, it yet conceals its sacred mystery.

"There are few indeed who understand the Truth of fire. Even so, it is this very Truth that I seek to share with you now."

At that instant he caused a spark to leap from the stones within his hands unto the wood at his feet; and having ignited the wood, he

61

continued speaking:

"Sister, have I not said unto you that all of Life is naught save light? Light vibrating at different speeds and so appearing in different forms.

"And have I not also said that within each particle of light there burns a sun, and that it is this very sun which creates the light?

"And so, Almitra, it is even now. For I joined these stones in my hand in such a way that I called forth a particle of light, causing it to share the fire of its sun."

"Thus the sun, which we see as the spark, flies to the wood. And with its song of heightened vibrations it calls unto the wood to leave behind the imprisoning slowness of the Earth forever, and join it in the ecstatic dance of light.

"The wood is stirred, entranced by this song and so, inspired by the spark it quickens itself, lifting from the Earth, and rises into the airy expanse of the sky.

"It rises and its pulse quickens until it can no longer contain the suns within it. And thus they soar forth as a flame to illumine our night.

"The sun within the stone is reunited with its kindred suns within the wood, and with great joy they join together to share their dance of

62

unity."

"And thus do not three apparently different things reveal their common nature? Ay,
for are not the spark, the wood and the flame
likened unto a single play which is enacted upon
three stages, revealing unto the viewer but a
central theme?

"Even so, Almitra, like unto the spark are
all of the prophets who have ever ministered
unto mankind. For have they not also come with
their quickening songs, calling unto all men and
women to release the confinement of their
smaller selves and rise into the limitless expanse
of the All-Self?

"Ay, for it is there that they shall recognize
all their brothers and sisters of the Earth as
being of that Self. And there also shall they join
together in the celebration of that unity."

"In this way, the prophets have sought for
naught save to join the whole of humanity
together, summoning them to experience and
appreciate the single creation which is Life.

"Yet, let us always remember that, because
of the nature of our being and our eternal gift of
free will, we each must personally receive the
call of the prophets. And, likewise, our response

must be personal as well.

"Ay, even as the prophets have foretold, at the moment of our reunion we stand truly alone with our Creator.

"And as all of Creation must respond, Almitra, so must you and I. Thus, let us merge our spirits within this flame, which even now dances upon the wood and illumines our night.

"And let us release our hearts unto each other's loving care and dance within this light, sharing the music and the joy of our unity."

Having spent four days amongst the mountains, we returned into the city upon the eve of the festival day.

And upon entering the Temple hall we were besought by a voice from within the shadows that said:

"Brother, I would speak with you."

Almustafa turned unto Jataz and held a lamp before him, saying:

"Ay, and I would gladly listen unto your words."

Upon hearing this, a calmness appeared about Jataz, and he said:

"Almustafa, I have come seeking a better understanding of your words, for they have echoed within the depths of my being since last we met, and I would come to believe them as you do.

"I have awaited you here so that I could ask

you to come and sit at my board, hoping that we may share the fruits of your learning while we share the fruits of my fields.

"And fear not, for I shall honor your decision to remain absent on the morrow. I but seek your presence on this eve alone."

Almustafa answered him, saying:

"Ay, Jataz, I shall sup with you and speak further of the light which moves within my mind and of the love which radiates from within my heart.

"For surely I would not deny you a clear understanding of the words that I have spoken. And perhaps, through your own understanding, those around you may come to understand.

"Let us pray that it may be so, for it is only through this agreement that we shall accept our brotherhood, and thus move beyond the walls of our supposed separate kinships."

As Jataz pondered over this, Almustafa turned toward me and said:

"Sister, release your anxious thoughts. Forever must we accept the gift of Life, and forever must we remember the essence of that gift: that every grain of Life throughout the whole of Creation is forever changing, forever

quickening the light within it. And so the Life
without quickens also.

"Remember, Almitra, that Life is one; and
it forever moves as one.

"Though someone would seek to harm us
one moment, we must enlarge our hearts to forgive such actions and move to accept that same
hand in love, perhaps in the following moment.

"For all of Life is eternally growing, and
there is naught in that growth save a moving
from darkness unto light, from fear unto love.

"And when that growth manifests itself
before us, we must nurture it with love, even as
others have nurtured our growth with that very
love.

"In this way we shall all rise together unto
the sun, perceiving the wonder of our origin,
realizing that all of Life is created as one and
that each of us manifests this unity according to
the compassion that reigns within our heart."

With these words he gently touched my
face, then turned toward Jataz. And together
they moved quietly out of the Temple.

Long into the night they supped, sharing the fruits of the fields and vines. With open ears, Jataz listened unto Almustafa as he spoke of Life and the unity thereof—and of the love which all must manifest if they are to share this unity in their hearts as well as in their lives.

Many words had passed between them when, of a sudden, Jataz leapt unto his feet and cried aloud, saying:

"Wrong have I been to think harm of you! And even more wrong have I been in seeking to harm you.

"Come! We must leave ere the ones who would harm you arrive and transport you into the night."

Almustafa besought him, saying:

"Speak further Jataz; explain your words."

Thus Jataz continued:

"When last we talked I was filled with fear,

69

for your words confused and amazed me. And so I spoke to the elders of the Temple, repeating for them all that you had spoken unto me; and it likewise kindled fear within their hearts.

"Thus, they had me bring you here in pretense of better understanding your words; but in truth they sought only to entrap you.

"For they gave me a flask of wine with a potion mixed into it, and of this wine I was to have you drink, causing you to fall deeply asleep. And so they would come and carry you away.

"Deep within the prison walls they would have taken you, but only for a few days; for they fear you and have not the courage nor the will to actually harm you.

"They but seek to silence you upon the Holy Day, for they did not believe in your absence on the morrow and thought in truth that you would appear to speak against them and their guests.

"And so, I have saved this wine until last; for as you spoke to me this evening my fear dissolved, as did my desire to serve their purpose.

"Forgive me, my brother, for the wrong I have done you. You, of all people, surely deserve no wrong."

Almustafa looked at him for a moment, and then he said:

"Always has it been, Jataz, that only in fear does one appear deserving of harm. For once the eyes are full of light, and so enabled to see the light, they see the Truth that all of Life deserves only love.

"We must come to view ourselves as gardeners in this sacred garden. We must plant with love and nurture with love, and when Life calls upon us, we shall weed with love.

"And finally, when all else is done, we shall harvest and partake of our fruits with love. And so, in truth, there is naught save love in all of our gardening.

"Brother, Life needs much more than the fruits of the fields to sustain it; Life can live only by love.

"Ay, Jataz, with this very love have I come and, likewise, with this very love shall I stay. Bring on this wine which conceals sleep within its kiss and fear not.

"For those who come do so only to escort me unto one who cries aloud for my presence. And I would partake of all manner of afflictions to sit at his side."

Thus, with hesitation and bewilderment,

Jataz brought forth the wine. In silence they emptied the flask into their cups and drank thereof until the last drop had disappeared between their lips, staining them crimson.

And as their heads began to nod in response to the potion, Almustafa turned toward Jataz and spoke to him:

"Sleep well my brother, and trouble not yourself with thoughts of concealment, nor your heart with guilt of trickery; for I say unto you that in truth you concealed naught from me this evening, nor did you ever trick me.

"Jataz, the only trickery throughout the whole of Life is fear. In fear we carve the mask of death upon our face and, likewise, with this very fear we bestow the dagger of our own death unto our executioners.

"This fear is the thief that would ravage our lives. And yet, even fear cannot enter in where it is not allowed entrance.

"And because I have encountered no fear this evening, I shall likewise encounter no harm. If you will but open your eyes this one last time you shall see a smile upon my face, stained by the kiss of the grape as deeply as your very own.

"So, did we not in truth share this wine in brotherhood and remembrance of our younger days, forgetting all else that may have come to pass?

"And did we not find ourselves unified as one within the Spirit, surrendering up unto the eternal fire of love and light all of the differences and distances which had come between us during our days of forgetfulness?

"Ay, Jataz, this we did and more. And in so doing, we came yet a little closer unto our higher Self.

"So sleep well, knowing that Life is ever with us, forever ensuring us of our safety and delivering us from our needs."

With these words floating into silence, both men bowed their heads in deep sleep.

And so they were when the priests came under the cloak of darkness to carry Jataz to bed and Almustafa to prison.

Almustafa awoke in total darkness, and yet he remained entirely at peace. Sitting quietly, he clothed himself within the brightness of his purpose.

And thus he lovingly called unto his heart to bring forth light before his eyes:

"Light of lights within my heart, fill this space which now surrounds me. Give forth your brilliance to guide my eyes, for they are blinded by this darkness.

"Ay, my Beloved, give forth your love and let there be light."

And so it was that a glowing orb of light surrounded Almustafa, enabling him to view his cell.

And it was with a love deep and full that he moved toward a man lying near him. Coming closer unto the man, Almustafa discovered him to be Nicodemus, a merchant he had known as a

75

youth.

With this recognition came a thankfulness that he had found the one whom he had sought; and so he called unto the sleeping man, saying:

"Greetings, Nicodemus, my brother of forgotten days. Peace be unto you."

With his mind full of sleep, Nicodemus turned his head toward Almustafa; and he said:

"Ay, Nicodemus is my name. And long have my ears hungered for the sound of that word spoken in kindness.

"Yet, wait a moment: do I dream? or were those words of this world? Who is it that speaks so unto me from out of the darkness?"

Almustafa answered him, saying:

"It is I, Almustafa, your brother from days long past. Do you remember naught of me? I was the youth who would come unto you and speak of the sacred workings of your heart and mind as we stood within the marketplace."

Nicodemus was silent for a space, and then he spoke with gladness in his words:

"Forgive me, Almustafa, for my eyes no longer serve me. But ay, well do I remember you. And in that remembrance there is sunlight to illumine my darkness and laughter to awaken my heart.

"What manner of man would confine you within this cell? Have your gentle ways changed to call forth this punishment against you?"

Almustafa reached forth his hand to touch Nicodemus, then answered him, saying:

"Nay, brother, my ways have not changed since last we met. And, in truth, no manner of man has imprisoned me here, although there are those who deem themselves to have done so.

"I but surrendered myself into the hands of those who would bring me unto you, for although I knew not the name of the one who called me, I know now. And so I am sitting here beside you.

"As for those who would imprison me, they deem themselves priests; yet they are not. For the true priests come clothed in light, and through the love in their hearts they bespeak the unity of Life and the freedom therein.

"Yet, these who call themselves priests know naught of freedom, nor would they have anyone be free. They would seek instead to imprison all who come before them within the desire to be free.

"Nicodemus, I say unto you that freedom unclaimed is indeed a prison; and love unfelt is indeed a fear."

"These men who parade around adorned in their golden robes do so only to entrance the people, seeking to amaze them with a show of earthly wealth.

"A beggar clad in naught but salvaged rags is more able to speak the Truth than they. They make their way from out of the darkness and say unto all that they come of the light.

"Brother, they come not out of love, save it be the love of power; and they come not in the light, save it be the light which reflects from the gold that they hoard."

"They speak their twisted words and say unto all that they speak for God. Yet, verily, they but juggle the words of our ancestors, weaving a net in which they seek to entrap all of Life.

"But truly, brother, Life is beyond all space and time; and no manner of trap shall ever hinder even the smallest portion of Life.

"Even those who preach the fear of a Oneness they know not would shine forth with the brilliance of the Sacred Light, could they but open their hearts unto the beauty of love."

"Ay, Nicodemus, could you but come alive to the Truth of Life, there would be no manner of prison that could contain you.

"For I say unto you that, even as you are imprisoned, you truly remain free before the face of the Infinite One. Could you but call that freedom into the center of your being it would dissolve your every prison.

"There are many who accept their imprisonment; but there are very few indeed who realize that this acceptance is their only real prison.

"Brother, forever does Life hold the key of release; you need but release unto Life to be given the key.

"Come, stand beside me now and share with me the loveliness and light of the morning sun."

Nicodemus answered him, saying:

"Almustafa, do you jest with an old man? Have I not said that my eyes are forever closed unto this world? And even more, are we not imprisoned within these walls and separated from the light of day?"

Almustafa embraced him with compassion as he answered, saying:

"Nay, brother, I make no jest of you. And ay, we are within this cell, hidden from the light of day; but we are not forsaken by the greater light, the Light of God.

"For it is this very Light which has filled this cell, giving me the gift of viewing your face.

"And likewise, even now that radiance fills my heart, calling upon the stones surrounding us to release us back into the light of day once more."

"Nicodemus, this cell is surely not our prison. For who amongst the many beings upon this Earth can deny the smallest portion of the sacredness of Life, or withdraw the holy gift of freedom that Life eternally bestows upon us?

"Verily there is none, for we are Life Divine; and the final decision eternally remains within each of us, to accept or refuse any experience which may come unto us."

Nicodemus besought Almustafa, and his voice quivered with awe as he said:

"Almustafa, what manner of man are you? Long have I lived upon this Earth, and yet I have met no one else who speaks of Life as you do. Would you tell an old man from what source you have obtained your wisdom?"

And Almustafa answered him:

"I am but a man, a man who walks hand in hand with Life. And thus I draw my wisdom from the very fount of Life.

"For what is it to become wise, but to wipe clear the mirror of the soul so that you may recognize therein your own divine countenance.

"And so, Nicodemus, I wear my manhood as a crown, whilst others scorn theirs as though it were a shroud.

"Yet Life sings within us all; within myself a song of fervent love for my Beloved; and within them a song of frozen fear of the great unknown.

"Gladly would I have every man and woman receive the Crown of Life, and so give back their shrouds unto the wind to return once more as dust unto the earth.

"Then would all be free to receive the love of Life and to leave this eternal fear of the harm which they believe Life seeks to do them."

Almustafa paused for a moment, looking deep within the eyes of Nicodemus. Then he continued, saying:

"Come Nicodemus, let us fashion from the light within this cell a crown for you to wear. For your eyes are but closed unto the darkness of this world, and they will gladly open again when filled with light.

"Let these words fill your heart with the light of love, and so fill your eyes with the light of day.

"And let us empty our minds of everything, save remembrance of our glorious Lord; and let us sing this song unto Him:

"My Lord, before all else was formed, You stood alone, clothed not in form, nourished by the Spirit Breath.

"Ay, You stood as does the dawning sun, resplendent in your nakedness.

"And yet, within that very nakedness was Your freedom to clothe Yourself with every shade of form.

"Even so, my Lord, it is Your loving hands, invisible to some, that silently uphold all others: living, dead, and yet unborn.

"And peacefully, my Lord, Your face smiles within all faces.

"While Your crystalline light illumines every darkness, flooding throughout the infinities of space.

"Ay, there is no place where Thou art not, no part of Life You do not touch.

"Lord of all Life, Thou art the Light.

"I pray Thee now—shine forth upon us."

Almustafa raised his eyes unto Nicodemus, and stood in humble joy as he watched his brother's transformation.

A blinding light had engulfed Nicodemus and, coursing swiftly through his form, it bathed his every atom. Merging with the pulsations of his heart and mind, it lovingly gave forth of its transforming clarity.

Thus quickened, he stood up trembling and with open, seeing eyes he spoke aloud unto the Lord:

"My Lord! Without you I am naught. You are the whole of my being.

"A barren lamp, I surrender myself unto You. And in Your glory, You rekindle my flame!"

It seemed that they stood still for eternity, letting these words vibrate throughout space until their echoes returned unto that silence from whence they came.

And having been touched by those subtle vibrations, both men rejoiced in their hearts.

Filled with elation, Almustafa turned unto Nicodemus and embraced him. Looking upon the tears in the old man's eyes, he said unto him:

"Welcome, Nicodemus; welcome into the garden of Life. And praised be the Lord of Life, for surely it was His radiant Love which clothed itself in this majestic light.

"Surely this is His Love, which winged its

way throughout the star-strewn spaces of the infinite universes and joyously transformed, with endless care, a creature of darkness into a Being of Light."

Nicodemus cried aloud with joy. And even through his tears he saw the glow of Almustafa's loving face, for his heart had filled with love and his eyes had filled with light.

Then Almustafa spoke:

"And now, my brother, let us call together upon the stones within this wall; and let us sing the quickening songs unto them, that we may leave this cell."

Nicodemus looked upon Almustafa with even deeper awe and amazement, and he said:

"Are you in truth counseling me to sing unto these stones? Would that we were stonecutters, and then perhaps we could sing a song unto them with our axes. But, brother, what may we do with naught save our hands?"

Almustafa stood before Nicodemus and answered him calmly, saying:

"In truth, we shall not even need our hands. For this wall is naught save particles of light, moving here so slowly as to appear immovable.

"But once it is quickened, as I shall now do, it will lose its hardness; and then we shall move through it as though we moved through air.

"Be not afraid, brother; open your mind and remember these words: there is naught in all of Creation that could confine or harm you once you realize the truth of vibration, and thus understand the Songs of Light."

"Ay, Nicodemus, I do indeed counsel you to sing a song of Light unto these stones, for by these very songs all of Life is guided.

"Light, the unnamed Lord of Life, sits upon the throne of all existence and, with a will both mighty and mysterious, rules the various realms of time and space.

"Throughout the whole of Creation, none shall gaze upon His beauty save the one who enters into His domain of Light. And no entrance into that land shall ever be, save through the Gate of Ecstatic Vibrations.

"There is none who shall know Him by force or cunning; and the ones who seek Him in those ways shall sleep beneath the ground long before they stand before His throne.

"But the humble ones who lovingly fill their beings with the delight of the Holy Spirit, they shall call unto the Lord by His various names.

"And He shall answer them and heed their needs.

"Ay, Nicodemus, and He shall heed our needs even now as I call upon Him. For it is He who sits within these stones and He also who shall escort us into the light of day."

With these words, Almustafa seated himself before the wall and began his song, calling unto the stones to quicken their energies and release the languor of the earth.

Nicodemus stood dumbfounded; for even though the song which Almustafa sang was silent, being not of this world, it did indeed cause movement within the stones.

And soon a portion of the wall began to fade. Upon this portion Almustafa blew with a strong breath, and it moved as a cloud being blown about in the wind.

And so Nicodemus and Almustafa walked through the space in the wall into the light of the morning sun. Nicodemus, witnessing the truth of their freedom, turned unto Almustafa and embraced him, breathlessly whispering:

"Ay, brother, now I see the beauty of the Lord of Light!"

Almustafa went straightway into the marketplace, while Nicodemus came to bring me word of their well being.

And so Almustafa was seen by the very priests who had carried him into the prison cell.

Quickly they called aloud unto others to gather and capture him; for they now were full afraid of him and would refrain from no action that would silence him.

As the circle of priests closed about him, Almustafa leapt upon a cart and called upon them, saying:

"Brothers, ere you act, hear my words."

Hafiz, an elder priest, shouted:

"We have heard of your words, Almustafa, and we have found them to be full of lies.

"Would that you had contained your words to speak unto the people only of themselves; instead you have filled their ears with idle

87

promises of unity with God.

"Perhaps you may lead children away into your land of dreams, but us you do not fool. So be silent!"

Almustafa raised his head and said:

"Rather should you attempt to silence the wind, for the Truths that I hold would be spoken.

"You say that I should have contained my words in speaking unto my brothers and sisters, speaking only of themselves and naught of their unity with God.

"And yet, I say unto you that I did indeed speak of naught save themselves when I spoke of God, for verily their larger Self is naught save God.

"Even so, I spoke of naught save the unity of the smaller and larger Selves, that in truth there is but one Self.

"And so I did indeed speak of unity with God, a unity which is not an idle promise, but an ever-present reality. For where else does God dwell if not also within our very being?

"And so we are One. And as we were in the beginning we shall continue to be, for our Life is without end."

"Even now as I speak we are bathed in the infinite love of God; and in so bathing us, He gathers us even further into the sublime Unity that is Himself.

"And as He gives unto us, He gives unto all; for there is naught within all of Creation that does not abide within the sacredness which we have named God.

"Ay, there does not move a particle of matter which exists as matter alone, for the whole of Creation exists first as a vibrating essence within the Holy Spirit.

"Even so, eternal and ever-joyous is God's love for all of Life. Given freely and fully unto all, He asks for nothing in return, for with His love is given also the royal gift of free will.

"Thus God leaves it unto each of us to choose how we shall return His love."

"Brothers, so have I spoken from the beginning and likewise speak even now. Yet, let not my words confuse you; better by far would it be to let His love refresh you.

"For those of you who hear my song in words alone, and feel naught of the love contained therein, are like unto those who hear the cry of the storm all around them, yet feel naught of the love with which it bathes the

Earth."

Hafiz interrupted him, saying:

"Silence, Almustafa! You feed us poetry. Do you seek to anger us?"

Almustafa turned to answer:

"Nay, brothers, I would have you pour naught of hatred into your hearts. For I say unto you that that which fills your heart shall likewise fill your days and nights; and that fear which seizes you for a moment shall plague you throughout your years.

"Rather would I have you fill your hearts with love, and so share with me our last embrace, for I go forth from you now as an arrow released from a bow. Ay, an arrow which even now quivers and prepares for flight."

Almustafa saw those within the crowd with whom he had shared his youth and his love, and he called unto them, saying:

"Come, my beloved ones, come unto me and share my touch. For it is with this touch that I give of myself, that I give of my love.

"And verily, I counsel you to go unto one another and realize that you stand united in the Spirit.

"And in the light of that union come to

understand the truth of the Living God, who is forever united throughout the infinity of time and space.

"One God, who heeds not the divisions that you would force upon Him, placing part of Him within the sky and another part within the earth, forever separate from Himself.

"The Lord heeds not those separations, for He emanates from every point of Life as a resplendent light."

And Hafiz cried: "Enough, enough!"

Then he turned toward the priests gathered around him and shouted:

"Silence this heretic! this wizard who defies stone walls. Let us release him back into his sacred light. Enough of his words to defile our Holy Day! Let us gather quickly and silence him now and forever!"

At these words I ran across the market square and stood near Almustafa, who turned toward me and said:

"Almitra, I am overjoyed that you have come, for we have much to share today.

"Open your sacred portal, my sister, and absorb the light of this moment. Bathe your entire being in this fountain and let it enable you to contain the fluid movement of the moment within the vessel of yourself.

"Verily, it is only then that you shall be prepared and able to serve as Life now calls upon you to serve.

"Ay, once clothed within this Light you shall become a sacred witness, and Life shall eternally preserve the memories which you now record within your mind."

"Record them with love, Almitra, for so shall they be shared with everyone who shall come seeking Life in my name, asking you to remember this day.

"And now, my sister of Light, go within yourself as you have ere now, and see me as that *I Am*.

"Come unto me and know that I am beyond all dualities such as pain and death. View this moment as you have viewed birth, as naught save the emergence of light into light.

"The unified Being in which we all have our existence has called me from within His Mind unto His Heart, and I go knowing full well that I shall return yet again unto His Mind."

Almustafa suddenly stood very still, as though time itself had frozen, and gazing deep into my eyes he shared his silent thoughts with me. And thus my fears vanished as I understood his words:

"My sister, look not upon these people as my murderers, for in truth I do not perish this day. I but continue upon my journey clad in a different form.

"And, Almitra, know you well that none sends me forth from this Earth one moment before my time. Even though the ones who stand before me now deem themselves to be the moving force, they are not.

"For verily all upon this Earth partake only of those movements which they have called upon themselves.

"And though the call seems silent at times, even unto their own ears, it is still heard by the ear of Life; and thus it is manifested by the hand of Life.

"And so it is with me even now. For in my movement am I still, and even in my going do I remain here with you, forever to speak of love and the joys of unity."

With the end of this silent song came a hail of stones that fell upon Almustafa.

He turned to face the priests and called upon the stones, saying:

"Gently brothers, softly, do you not yet remember? It is I, Almustafa, your brother from years past. I am the one who, not so very long ago, would stop amidst my thoughtful steps to lift many of you from the loving arms of our mother Earth.

"With these very hands I lifted you closer unto my eyes, to drink of your beauty, and to marvel at the mysteries which you are.

"Ay, my friends, this and more have I done; for was I not the one who exulted at your life when all others deemed you cold, dead stone?

"Remember, my silent brothers, and dance lightly upon my skin; for verily I need naught of your kiss upon this flesh to rise beyond this form. I need only release unto Life to dance upon the wind."

His words ended as he collapsed beneath a heavy shroud of stones, and I stood riveted as his voice returned yet again into the air.

In the music of his words was the wind of a great star passing; and he said:

"You may cover my eyes with this layer of dust, but you shall never dim the light which shined within them."

95

As his words faded, there appeared amidst the stones a light between his eyes. It formed a circle upon his skin, then floated into the air, the sphere of a universe pulsing with Life.

The light rose swiftly into the sky, drifting and swirling within the currents of the air, forming the image of a man—a man so vast that he contained the sky.

And yet he stood in space with arms of mist outstretched toward the ones below, the very ones who stood upon the Earth and continued to stone the earthly form of the spirit being, Almustafa, the chosen and the beloved.

While, in truth, the master of that house had already departed from the body that so lovingly had carried him throughout his days on Earth, into realms and ages of which they had yet to dream.